DECOUPAGE

To Nilo

A WARD LOCK BOOK

First published in the UK 1996
by Ward Lock
Wellington House
125 Strand
LONDON
WC2R OBB

A Cassell Imprint

Distributed in the United States
by Sterling Publishing Co., Inc.
387 Park Avenue South, New York, NY 10016-8810

Distributed in Australia
by Capricorn Link (Australia) Pty Ltd
2/13 Carrington Road, Castle Hill NSW 2154

A British Library Cataloguing in Publication Data block for this book may be obtained from the British Library.

ISBN 0 7063 7462 2
Typeset by Art
Printed and bound in Italy

M. Macchiavelli

DECOUPAGE

IDEAS AND PROJECTS TO DECORATE YOUR HOME

WARD LOCK

CONTENTS

INTRODUCTION 6
The history of decoupage 7

TECHNIQUE 9

MATERIALS 10
Notes on cutting out 12
Types of paper 13

METHODS 18
Paintbrush method 19
Spray method 20
First mixed method 20
Second mixed method 20

PROJECTS 23

Wooden chopping board 24
Clock 28
Tray 32
Salt and pepper pots 36
Terracotta dish 40
Plate 44
Heart-shaped box 48
Shoe-box 52
Watering can 56

Lacquered saucer 60
Sugar container 64
Rubber boots 68
Lampshade 72
Glass dish 76

IDEAS 81

Small round table 82
Octagonal card table 83
Porcelain dish 84
Oval box 85
Writing desk set 86
Paperknife 86
Writing folder 86
Pencil box 88
Pen holder 88

Magnifying glass 88
File 89
Trays 90
Dishes 92
Wooden table 94
Christmas baubles 96
Decorated eggs 97
Candles 97
Small tray 98
Milk jug 100
Small chocolate tray 100
Water sprinkler 101
Shoe-brush box 102
Terracotta plate 104
Chair 105

Oval box 106
Wooden casket 107
Round boxes 108

ENGLISH STYLE 110

Tray 112
Picture frames 114
Coat hanger 116
Knitting needle box
or tie box 116
Chairs 117
Decorative ball 118
Bellows 119
Wooden boxes 120
Mantelpiece clock 123

DECOUPAGE AND CARTOONS 125

Wall clock 126
Folding chair 128
Picture frame 129

AMERICAN STYLE 131

Picture frame 133
Low bench 134
Clothes hanger 135

ARTIST'S DECOUPAGE 137

DECORATIONS FOR DECOUPAGE 147

INTRODUCTION

When I was six or seven years old cutting out pictures from magazines was one of my favourite pastimes. I would go into the cupboard where my mother kept old magazines (in those days we did not throw anything away) and I would choose the ones with the largest number of pictures. I loved photographs and usually discarded those with too many drawings. I would spend hours cutting out pictures and when my pile of cuttings was ready, I would dip them in a bowl of water and then stick them, just as they were, onto the doors of our white kitchen sideboard.

I called this the cinema game. It is not surprising that this early memory came so clearly to mind when I agreed to prepare this book.

In fact, I have become a designer, both to earn a living and for pleasure. Decoupage is one of the many decorative techniques that I have been using for several years now. I have always regarded it as a minor technique, but being reminded of my childhood game has made me appreciate why I have developed this recent passion, which has prompted me to put down my pencils and paintbrushes and pick up scissors and cutters.

Developing my own personal technique for stabilizing my collages has been a great help. Knowing that I could carry out infinite overlapping of cuttings on all types of surface and make them waterproof and vitrified, has left my imagination free to roam at will.

Because, in the end, this is the main characteristic of decoupage, quite apart from different and personalized working methods: the infinite ways of expressing one's creativity without having to learn a complex technique, as you do for sketching and painting.

In the technical part of the book I have described 14 applications of this method following the guidelines of recipe books. However, these are clearly a pretext for

6

Couple of French walnut palettes, decorated with decoupage figures (ca. 1870).

a detailed description of the materials and not a strict working method. Perhaps these descriptions are a little too didactic, but there is nothing worse than vagueness in a manual.

I have tried to be clear and direct, mainly in order to transmit the desire to create. your own original designs. My idea is that everyone should develop his or her own style, according to taste and personality.

THE HISTORY OF DECOUPAGE

Decoupage, from the French verb *découper* which means 'to cut out', refers to the technique by which surfaces are decorated with pictures of cut-out paper, applied and vitrified using various types of transparent varnish. There is no real data about the origins of this practice of decoupage.

Man has most probably developed the use of cuttings ever since paper was first created.

The first definite references to decoupage date from the Middle Ages, when strips of water-coloured paper were attached to the walls and when monks used gilded and finely engraved paper to decorate miniatures. However the first furniture and objects decorated with paper cuttings and lacquered, arrived in Europe from the East in the sixteenth century. The technique was therefore rediscovered and, in the seventeenth century, the European courts were literally inundated with lacquered objects and pieces decorated with decoupage silhouettes. Even Marie Antoinette amused herself by practising the noble art of decoupage. The technique became generalized and widespread in England during the nineteenth century, mainly due to the fashion for print rooms (generally the antechambers of libraries), which were entirely decorated with posters and paper picture frames applied directly to the walls. Furniture and objects made in painted or unpainted wood began to be produced with decorations of posters cut into 'ribbons': frames, ribbons, bows, cherubs and roses. The wood was finished with layers and layers of lacquered glue.

This method was obviously exported to America and realized by putting together the most banal pictures. Collages of tropical flowers, pin-ups and postcards of Florida were the inspiration of the 1950s, and this is the type of decoupage that has generally come back into fashion.

Decoupage, as you can see from this potted history, has evolved to produce a number of very different styles, from chic and sophisticated to jazzy and modern. Interpret these to suit your own taste and decorative style.

TECHNIQUE

MATERIALS

Decoupage can be made on more or less any type of surface, and that really means on anything at all! In theory, a whole house could be decorated with decoupage, from the walls to furniture and household goods.

Obviously not all surfaces produce the same effect. Wood, for example, particularly rough wood, that has not been treated with varnishes or wood sealers, is the ideal surface. The fact that the glue penetrates into the pores creates perfect adhesion between the paper cuttings and the surface to which they are attached. Then, once the varnish has been spread with a brush, for example using the various coats in the English way, you can no longer feel the difference in thickness between paper and wood, even when passing your hand across the decorated surface.

Anyway, with a small amount of practice and experimentation, you can manage to decorate almost anything.

Rough wood, wood treated with transparent varnish, rough cardboard, cardboard covered in glossy paper, natural terracotta and stretched material show how easy it is to create successful decoupage on a variety of wood and paper surfaces.

*Non-lacquered metal
(aluminium, iron,
copper, steel, pewter
etc.), painted
(lacquered) metal,
solid wax (candles),
transparent
and coloured stiff
plastic and rubber
are all suitable.*

*White porcelain,
white and coloured
ceramics, terracotta,
transparent glass
and perspex all
make elegant bases
for decoupage.*

NOTES ON CUTTING OUT

There are no particular secrets to learn as far as the cutting out is concerned. Although it certainly is an art in itself, it is also a question of practice. Obviously, the tools of the trade are extremely important. Before you start, you need to be equipped with a pair of sharp scissors suitable for this kind of work, preferably in different sizes.

Long-blade scissors for cutting large sheets of paper.
Medium-sized scissors for curved surfaces and *manicure* or *embroidery work scissors* for small detail.

You also need a *cutter*. There are some highly sophisticated models with curved or adjustable blades but perhaps the most suitable type is a simple narrow-bladed cutter, with interchangeable blades. It is important to cut away the used section of the blade frequently, so that it is always very sharp. When using the cutter you should protect your work surface, either with a special wooden cutting board or simply a sheet of glass with the edges covered with sticky tape. Tidiness is essential. When cutting, you should always place the cuttings on a tray which will allow you to try out various designs, especially if the pieces are very small. I would also suggest that, while you are cutting out, you try to maintain a smooth, harmonious movement of the scissors and the paper. This helps to keep the edges straight and even.

TYPES OF PAPER

One of the questions that I am most frequently asked is: 'Where do you find all these beautiful paper designs?' I manage to express my enthusiasm for decoupage in my search for paper. In fact the beautiful paper is usually under our noses and we only need to use our imagination in order to discover it.

In the two photographs which follow there is a collection of materials from which I generally take my cuttings. Here is a list, by way of explanation.

MAGAZINES OF ALL KINDS. Glossy and opaque. Fashion, cooking, travel and news magazines.

OLD MAGAZINES. Those you find in flea markets or attics.

COMICS AND CHILDREN'S MAGAZINES.

OLD AND NEW MUSICAL SCORES.

DOVER BOOKS. These are a real treasure for decoupage. In fact, this English publishing house has reprinted quite cheaply an enormous number of ink drawn pictures of Victorian designs. They are generally books on a particular theme: birds, children, food and drink, horses and flowers, for example. The books only contain pictures and, if you do not use the books themselves (which would be rather a shame!), you can use photocopies.

WRAPPING PAPER. Beautiful wrapping paper has recently been produced, printed with a great variety of attractive designs. The best stationery shops have very original types and, even if they may be a little expensive, one sheet can give you an enormous number of cuttings.

PHOTOCOPIES. This is the secret of modern decoupage. Photocopies, especially of those famous Dover books, of musical scores, of pages from newspapers or famous books are enormously useful. You can use white or coloured paper. Photocopying paper is also particularly suited to gluing.

COLOUR PHOTOCOPIES. These are still expensive and a colour photocopier is not always easy to find. However, they are an excellent solution if you have very beautiful pictures and you do not want to use originals. Surprisingly, the copies are often more beautiful than the originals.

POSTCARDS AND PHOTOGRAPHS. These can only be applied to smooth surfaces.

PREPARED VICTORIAN CUTTINGS. These have recently come onto the market, specifically designed for decoupage. They are highly colourful reproductions of small nineteenth century pictures, generally already cut on embossed paper. They are not easy to find, are a little difficult to apply and are all roughly the same size, so working with this material alone could be a little monotonous. However, it is extremely useful when combined with other types of pictures.

OTHER EXAMPLES: old family photographs; stamps; dried and pressed leaves; wine labels; lace-work and anything else which is very thin and can be glued.

From top left: Dover Books with old Victorian prints, optical and tartan designs.
In the centre: old magazines from the 1950s and 1960s, for cutting or photocopying, musical scores and, underneath these, pages of printed silhouettes. Finally, below: modern fashion and news magazines and books of cartoons.

From top left: series
of decorated
wrapping papers
printed on matt
paper, all with highly
suitable subjects
for decoupage
(architectural
designs, dogs, roses
and leaves).
In the centre, over
the wrapping paper:
illustrated postcards
with photographs
of roses.
From bottom left:
a whole series
of photocopied
pictures, in black
and white, both
on white
and coloured paper,
as well as colour
photocopies. These
include pages from
musical scores,
pages from Dover
Books, pictures
from art books
and from an old
Victorian calendar.

METHODS

Among all the people I know who make decoupage objects, none of them use exactly the same method to solidify and water-proof their work.

As in all types of craftsmanship, everyone finds their own true balance between material, time and method, with the help of experience. Therefore, what I am about to describe is not *the* method, but *my* method. You will no doubt develop your own.

Decorating a surface with decoupage means attaching paper cuttings to the surface, *isolating* them and, finally, covering them with a transparent protective finish.

For this technique, emphasis must be placed on the word 'isolating'. In fact, if cuttings are stuck onto a wooden box and the varnish is then immediately applied, the oily base of the latter will penetrate the paper and cause permanent damage.

Therefore, the secret is to plasticize the paper in some way. The simplest and most efficient method is that of gluing both surfaces of the cuttings, both the top and the underside of the pictures.

Once dry, the glue becomes transparent and the paper stretches if it has been creased when wet.

Then the varnish can be applied and will no longer filter through the pores of the paper. Using various coats of varnish the paper shapes will be perfectly amalgamated, becoming an integral part of the surface.

To carry out this process I use two methods, which I call: the *paintbrush method and* the *spray method*, as well as two variations of these methods.

To illustrate my methods more clearly I have photographed what I use for each of the four methods, to which I will also refer in the technical notes which follow.

PAINTBRUSH METHOD

Dilute vinyl glue with a little water. The proportion should generally be 1 to 5: one spoonful of water to five of glue. It is important that it should neither be too sticky nor too liquid.
Mix it well with the paintbrush.
Apply glue to both surfaces of your back and front cuttings, place them on your surface and let them dry completely, for 2 to 3 hours.
Apply a coat of varnish with a paintbrush. After 5 or 6 hours you can apply a second coat, then a third or fourth coat, and so on.
Clean the varnish brush with turpentine and then wash it in soapy water.

NOTE: This is a universal method, which can be used on any surface and is cheap, although it is slower than other methods.

What you need:
- scissors and cutter
- vinyl glue
- paintbrushes
  for the glue
- container
  for diluted glue
- water
- gloss or satin-finish
  varnish
- paintbrush
  (to spread
  the varnish)
- turpentine

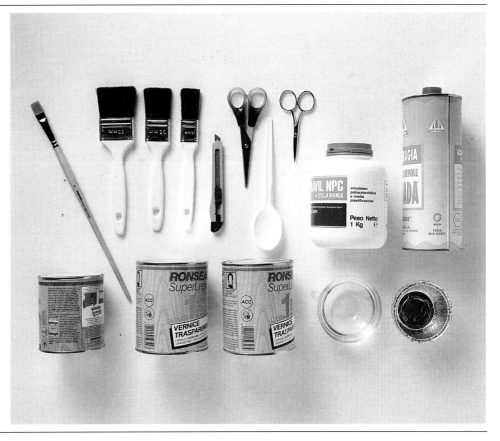

SPRAY METHOD

While protecting your work surface with paper or newspaper, spray the back of your cuttings with spray glue.
Apply them to the surface and flatten them with your hands. When you do this always put a piece of white paper between your hands and the cuttings.
Spray the acrylic fixative spray onto the paper cuttings.
Leave to dry for 10-15 minutes.
Now that you have isolated your paper, spray with the spray varnish.
Wait for 20 minutes before spraying a second coat.

NOTE: This method is much quicker than the paintbrush method, but also much more expensive. You must take great care not to breathe in the spray; always work in a well-aired environment.

What you need:
- scissors and cutter
- permanent adhesive spray glue (which can be bought in stationery and art shops)
- acrylic spray fixative for charcoal pencil drawings (found in paint and stationery shops)
- gloss or matt spray varnish

FIRST MIXED METHOD

Apply spray glue to the cuttings, isolate them with fixative and apply the varnish with a paintbrush.

SECOND MIXED METHOD

Paste the cuttings with vinyl glue. Spread the glue over the cuttings and wait until the surface is completely dry. Cover with transparent spray varnish.

What you need:
- scissors and cutter
- permanent
  adhesive spray
  glue
- acrylic spray
  fixative for
  drawings
- gloss
  or satin-finish
  varnish
- paintbrush
  to spread
  the varnish
- turpentine

What you need:
- scissors and cutter
- vinyl glue
- aluminium
  container
  for the glue
- water
- paintbrush
  to spread
  the glue
- gloss or matt
  spray varnish

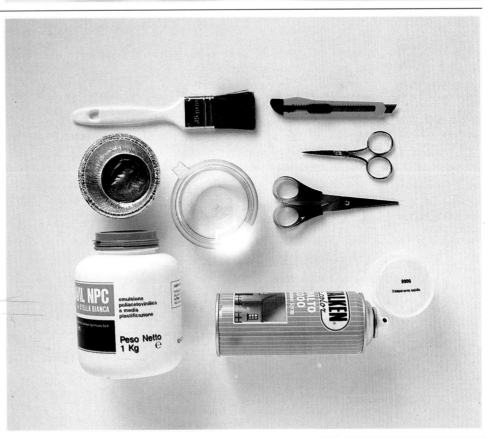

PROJECTS

WOODEN CHOPPING BOARD

METHOD: Paintbrush
OBJECT: Small chopping board for cold meats
or vegetables
MATERIAL: Rough wood

CHARACTERISTICS OF THE MATERIAL: Rough wood is certainly the most
suitable surface for decoupage. The untreated open pores of the
wood absorb the glue perfectly, offering ideal adhesion for the
paper. If several layers of varnish are then applied, the
cuttings seem to fuse with the wood forming a smooth
and even surface.

NOTES ON WHAT YOU NEED: The wooden
chopping board, new or old, can be
used on the undecorated side. The
cut-out leaves in the picture
have been taken from a
piece of non-glossy
wrapping
paper.

What you need:
- wooden chopping
  board
- wrapping paper
  with printed leaves
- medium-blade
  scissors
- cutter
- vinyl glue
- small flat
  paintbrush
  for the glue
- aluminium
  container
  for the glue
- gloss varnish
- paintbrush
  for the varnish
    - turpentine

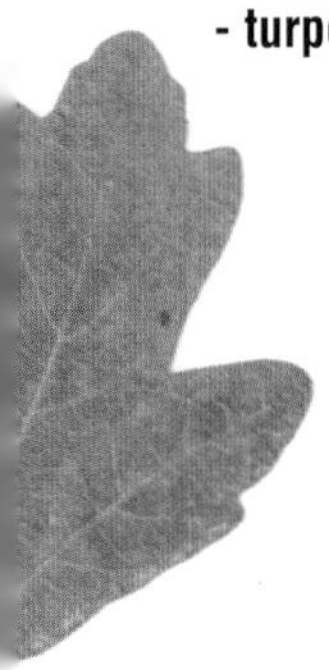

Carefully cut out
about 10 leaves
or more, according
to the dimensions
of the leaves
and the size
of your board.

Using a piece
of paper to protect
your work surface,
spread the glue
on the back
of each leaf.

Create your leaf
design, applying
the leaves
to the chopping
board.
Then cover
the whole surface
with glue, including
the parts with
no cuttings.

When the glue has
dried, i.e. when
the surface is
totally transparent
once more, apply
a coat of gloss
varnish. After
5 or 6 hours
you can apply
a second coat.

CLOCK

METHOD: Paintbrush
OBJECT: Clock
MATERIAL: Cleaned and treated rough
wood

CHARACTERISTICS OF THE MATERIAL: This is a piece
of plywood, shaped using a household saw and with
a hole in the centre. It has been dipped
in acrylic paints, that is, painted with
colours that have been considerably
diluted with water so that the grain
of the wood is still visible. Paint
applied in this way does not
completely close the pores of the
wood, so decoupage is still easily
done, as on rough wood.

NOTES ON WHAT YOU NEED: In
this case, the most difficult parts
to obtain are the metal circle
with the numbers and movements
of the clock, which can be found
in specialized shops. Alternatively,
you can use parts of an old clock.
The cuttings come from colour
photocopies of a calendar
decorated with roses
and Victorian fashion-plates.

What you need:
- piece of multi-layered plywood 8-10 mm thick
- acrylic water-colours for wood: salmon pink, yellow ochre, gold
- ageing finish
- metal circle with clock numbers
- quartz clock mechanisms
- colour photocopies of Victorian flowers and figures
- small scissors
- vinyl glue
- small flat paintbrush for the glue
- aluminium container for the glue
- satin-finish varnish
- paintbrush for varnish
- turpentine
- small paintbrush with a round point for the decoration

Pour a small quantity
of salmon pink
and yellow ochre
acrylic paint
into two saucers.
With a flat,
wet brush paint
the wood, mixing
the colours directly
on the surface.

Allow the paint to dry
while you cut out the
roses and Victorian
fashion-plates. Make
the decoration by
gluing the cuttings
on both sides. Cover
the whole surface
of the wood
with vinyl glue.

When the glue has dried completely, cover with a layer of satin-finish varnish.

After a few hours cover with a thin layer of ageing finish using a cloth. Mount the clock face, the mechanism and the hands and complete with small brush stroke decorations using the gold paint.

TRAY

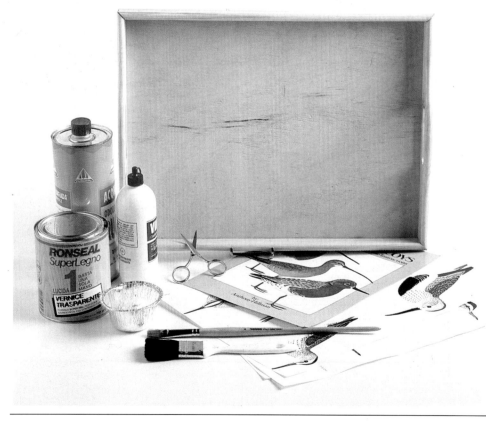

METHOD: Paintbrush
OBJECT: Tray
MATERIAL: Polished wood

CHARACTERISTICS OF THE MATERIAL: It is more difficult to attach
the cuttings to polished wood, as opposed to rough wood. It is important
to keep applying glue to the points where it tends to disappear.
As for the finish, an acrylic gloss varnish was used to give the same
effect as traditional varnishes, although it dries much more quickly
and can be diluted with water. Besides, it can be spread directly on the wood
without needing a base.

NOTES ON WHAT YOU NEED: A rough wooden tray which can easily be found
in do-it-yourself shops. The bird cuttings are colour photocopies taken
from a book about birds.

What you need:
- rough wooden
  tray
- pine-green
  acrylic gloss
  paint
- colour
  photocopies
  of pictures
  of birds
- small scissors
- vinyl glue
- small flat
  paintbrush
  for the glue
- aluminium
  container
  for the glue
- gloss varnish
- paintbrush
  for the varnish
- turpentine

Spread the acrylic paint directly onto the wood (it does not need a base). Wait for half an hour and then spread a second layer of paint.

Allow the paint to dry completely (for about 2 hours). Cut out the bird figures carefully and spread vinyl glue on the back of the cuttings.

Make your design
on the surface
of the tray
and then cover
the whole surface
of the tray
with vinyl glue.

When the glue is
completely dry,
cover with the first
coat of varnish.
After 5 or 6 hours,
add a second coat.

SALT AND PEPPER POTS

METHOD: Second mixed method
OBJECT: Salt and pepper pots
MATERIAL: White porcelain

CHARACTERISTICS OF THE MATERIAL: Porcelain
is a surprisingly successful surface for decoupage.
In fact, despite its extremely smooth finish, the glue sticks
perfectly and the cuttings can be flattened quite easily. The only
variation in method regards the varnish. Varnish applied with a paintbrush
tends to become yellowed with age on very white surfaces, so it is sometimes
preferable to use spray varnish, which remains perfectly transparent.

NOTES ON WHAT YOU NEED: The couple of common white porcelain salt
and pepper pots are enlivened and made more original by the application
of fruit pictures from the 1950s taken from a magazine.

What you need:
- porcelain salt and pepper pots
- stick-on pictures of fruit
- small scissors
- cutter
- vinyl glue
- small flat paintbrush for the glue
- aluminium container for the glue
- gloss spray varnish

Cut the flowers out very carefully. The object you are working on is very small so any imperfections will be noticeable.

Using a piece of paper to protect your work surface, spread the glue on the back of each cutting.

Stick the cuttings to the porcelain, making them adhere well by covering the whole surface of the pots repeatedly with glue.

When the glue is completely dry (the surface will be transparent and slightly glossy once more), spray with gloss varnish. After half an hour you can spray a second coat. Remember to work in a well-aired environment.

TERRACOTTA DISH

METHOD: Spray (to be applied in a well-aired room)
OBJECT: Terracotta dish
MATERIAL: Rough terracotta

CHARACTERISTICS OF THE MATERIAL: Terracotta, if it is not glazed, is a highly porous substance. It may be a little difficult to attach the shapes with the spray glue but persevere.

NOTES ON WHAT YOU NEED: This is a common flower-pot dish used as a base for standing pots in.
Cuttings: Watches are among the objects most frequently publicized and photographed in every type of magazine (women's, men's, news magazines etc.); so all you need to do is collect a few magazines to obtain your material for the decoupage.

What you need:
- terracotta garden flower-pot dish
- magazines and newspapers
- small-blade scissors
- permanent spray glue
- acrylic spray fixative for charcoal pencil drawings
- gloss spray varnish

Carefully cut out about thirty pictures of watches – the number will vary according to the size of the photographs and how big you want the images on the pot to be.

Using a piece of paper to protect your work surface, spray the glue onto each cutting and start to make your collage. Smooth down the cuttings in order to make them adhere completely to the surface, placing a piece of white paper between your hands and the cuttings while you press.

When you have
finished your design,
spray a coat
of charcoal-drawing
fixative to waterproof
the paper.

After half an hour
the fixative will be
dry and you can
lacquer the surface
of the flower-pot dish
with gloss spray
varnish.

PLATE

METHOD: Second mixed method
OBJECT: Plate
MATERIAL: Coloured ceramic

CHARACTERISTICS OF THE MATERIAL:
Ceramic, like porcelain, is a highly
suitable surface for decoupage. Be
careful how you spread the varnish
with the paintbrush (individual
brush strokes should not be
visible) and, in the case
of white ceramics, it is
always better to use
spray so that no
yellowing occurs.

NOTES ON WHAT YOU
NEED: Dark blue
ceramic dish, with
decorations inspired
by Fornasetti designs.
The Milanese artist,
Fornasetti, created
a style of decoration
based on eighteenth
century etchings.
The photocopy of the
eighteenth century
engraving was
taken from a book
of illustrations
of children.

What you need:
- coloured ceramic dish
- photocopy of an engraving of a child's face
- medium-blade scissors
- vinyl glue
- small flat paintbrush for the glue
- aluminium container for the glue
- gloss spray varnish

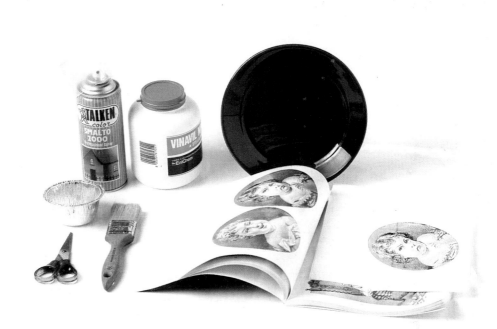

Cut the photocopy out carefully. Since it is a single round design try to cut around smoothly, leaving no edges.

Spread the glue on the back of the cutting.

Place it carefully in the centre of the plate and spread the glue over the design and over the whole surface of the plate.

Leave the glue to dry and, when the surface is transparent once more, spray with varnish. Remember to work in a well-aired environment.

HEART-SHAPED BOX

METHOD: Paintbrush
OBJECT: Heart-shaped box
MATERIAL: Rough cardboard

CHARACTERISTICS OF THE MATERIAL: Rough cardboard is quite similar to natural wood. It is an excellent surface for the glue. It obviously has to be very well isolated so that the varnish cannot penetrate and leave grease marks.

NOTES ON WHAT YOU NEED:
Heart-shaped boxes are not always easy to find but a well-stocked gift or stationery shop should be able to provide you with one. The flower cuttings are black and white photocopies taken from a book on flowers.

What you need:
- rough cardboard
  box
- black-and-white
  photocopies taken
  from a book
  on flowers
- medium-blade
  scissors
- cutter
- vinyl glue
- small flat
  paintbrush
  for the glue
- aluminium
  container
  for the glue
- gloss varnish
- paintbrush
  for the varnish
- turpentine

Cut the photocopied flowers out very carefully with the cutter.

Spread the glue on the back of the cuttings and attach them to the top and sides of the box.

Cover the cuttings carefully with a layer of glue and then cover the whole surface with glue, including the parts with no cuttings.

When the glue has dried completely (when the surface is totally transparent once again), apply the first coat of gloss varnish. After 4 or 5 hours you can add a second coat.

SHOE-BOX

METHOD: Spray (to be applied in a well-aired room)
OBJECT: Shoe-box
MATERIAL: Cardboard covered with gloss coated paper

CHARACTERISTICS OF THE MATERIAL: This is a way to use old boxes. Any type of box can be used: shoe-boxes, shirt-boxes etc. These boxes are generally covered with glossy paper. This blocks the effect of the glue a little but, once the cuttings have adhered, excellent results can be obtained.

NOTES ON WHAT YOU NEED: As for the watch-decorated terracotta dish (see page 40), photographs of perfume can be found in many different types of magazine.

What you need:
- well-preserved
  shoe-box
- magazines
- medium-blade
  scissors
- permanent spray
  glue
- acrylic spray
  fixative
  for charcoal
  pencil drawings
- matt spray varnish

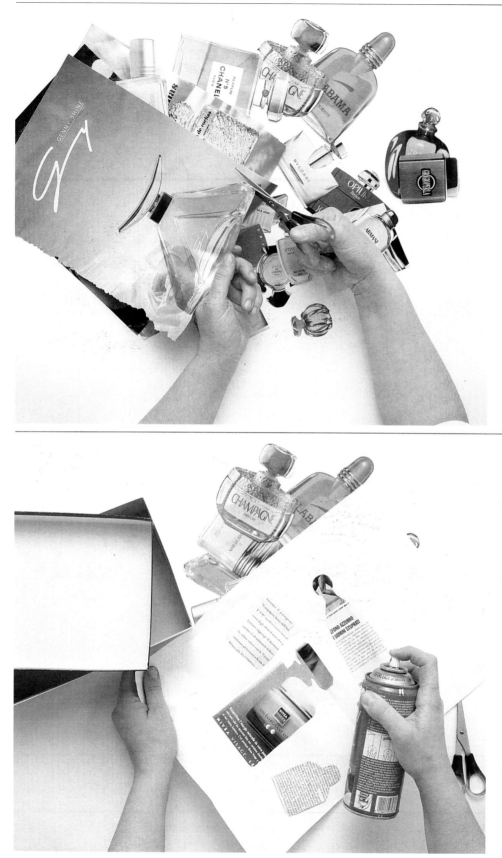

Cut out large
and small pictures
of perfume bottles
from newspapers
and magazines.

Using a piece of card
to protect your work
surface, spray the
glue onto the back
of the cuttings. Apply
them to the box,
making an
overlapping design.

When you have finished your collage, spray a generous coat of acrylic fixative onto the design to waterproof the paper completely.

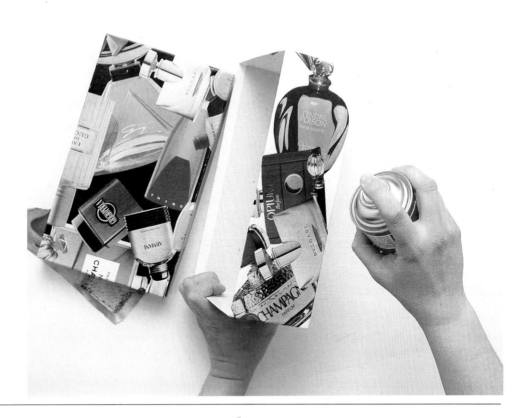

When the fixative is dry, spray the surface with matt varnish.

WATERING CAN

METHOD: Paintbrush
OBJECT: Watering can
MATERIAL: Aluminium

CHARACTERISTICS OF THE MATERIAL:
Aluminium, like all other metals, can be
decorated with decoupage. The vinyl
glue may shrink a little when it is applied but,
once dry, this effect should no longer be noticeable.

NOTES ON WHAT YOU NEED: If the watering can is
treated with two or three coats of varnish, it should
be possible to continue to use it for watering, since
it will be perfectly waterproof.

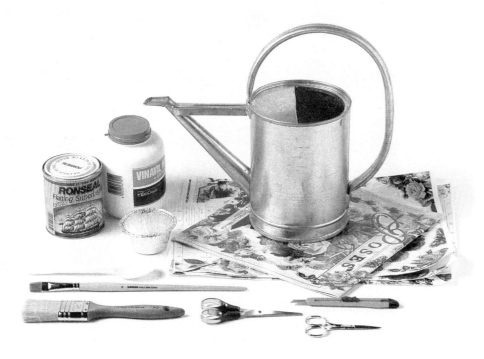

What you need:
- aluminium
  watering can
- colour
  photocopies from
  a rose-decorated
  calendar
- medium
  and small-blade
  scissors
- cutter
- vinyl glue
- aluminium
  container
  for the glue
- small flat
  paintbrush
  for the glue
- gloss boat varnish
- paintbrush
  for the varnish
- turpentine

Cut the colour photocopies of roses, butterflies and bows out very carefully.

Glue the shapes onto the watering can in the position you want them.

Cover the whole surface of the watering can with vinyl glue, flattening the cuttings carefully with the brush.

When the glue has dried completely (in 2 or 3 hours), apply the first coat of varnish. After 5 hours the surface will be dry enough to add a second coat of varnish.

LACQUERED SAUCER

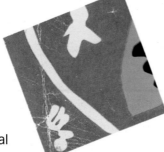

METHOD: Paintbrush
OBJECT: Saucer
MATERIAL: Lacquered metal

CHARACTERISTICS OF THE MATERIAL: Lacquered metal, like metal with
a natural finish, is not difficult to decorate with decoupage. Varnish
spread with a paintbrush can alter the smoothness of the finish a little.
Since the brush strokes will be visible, it is best to apply only one coat
of varnish.

NOTES ON WHAT YOU NEED: The pictures used for the cuttings are colour
photocopies taken from a book of reproductions of works by Matisse.
This type of saucer can easily be bought in supermarkets and shops
selling household goods.

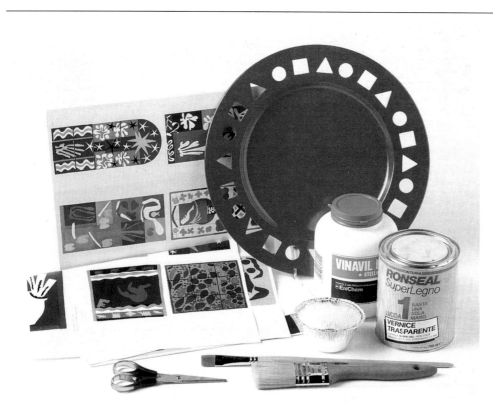

What you need:
- lacquered metal
  saucer
- colour
  photocopies
  of postcards
  of works
  by Matisse
- medium-blade
  scissors
- vinyl glue
- small flat
  paintbrush
  for the glue
- aluminium
  container for the
  glue
- gloss varnish
- flat paintbrush
  for the varnish
- turpentine

*Cut the colour
photocopies out.*

*Glue the backs
of your cuttings
and arrange them
on the saucer.*

Cover the cuttings
and the whole surface
of the saucer
with vinyl glue.

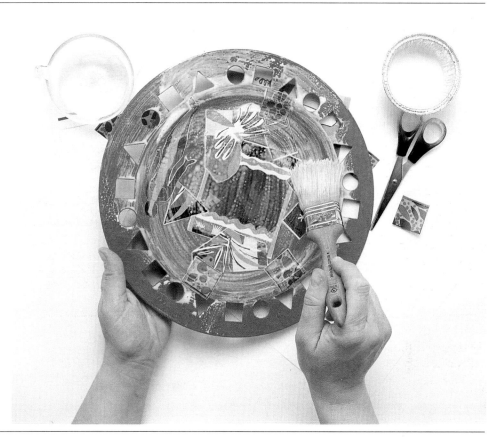

When the glue is
completely dry, apply
the first coat of
transparent varnish
with the brush. It is
best to apply only
one coat to prevent
yellowing with age.

SUGAR CONTAINER

METHOD: Paintbrush
OBJECT: Sugar or salt container
MATERIAL: Stiff transparent plastic

CHARACTERISTICS OF THE MATERIAL: Transparent plastic is perhaps the most difficult material to decorate with decoupage. In fact, the vinyl glue tends to shrink a lot when it is applied so you must brush over it many times to make it spread.
The varnish, especially in the case of transparent plastic, risks making the object turn yellow. Therefore, again it is best to apply only one coat.

NOTES ON WHAT YOU NEED: The cuttings are photocopies from a book on Victorian kitchen utensils.

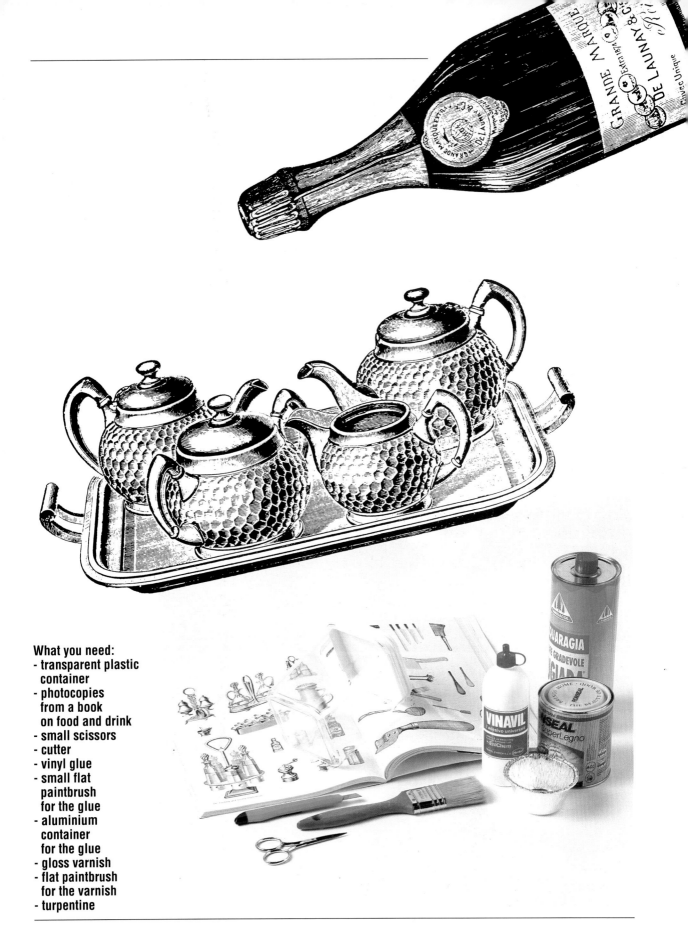

What you need:
- transparent plastic container
- photocopies from a book on food and drink
- small scissors
- cutter
- vinyl glue
- small flat paintbrush for the glue
- aluminium container for the glue
- gloss varnish
- flat paintbrush for the varnish
- turpentine

Cut the photocopied pictures out, using the cutter to help you follow the exact outlines.

Glue the backs of your cuttings.

Arrange the pictures on the container and cover them and the whole surface of the container with vinyl glue.

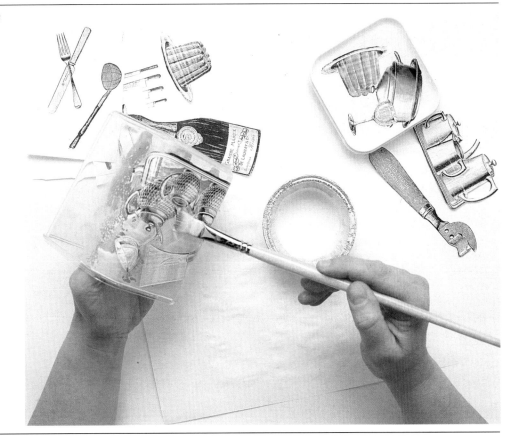

When the glue is completely dry, apply one coat of varnish.

RUBBER BOOTS

METHOD: Paintbrush
OBJECT: Rubber boots
MATERIAL: Rubber

CHARACTERISTICS OF THE MATERIAL: Rubber is the most challenging material for decoupage. Difficulties can be overcome by spreading a large amount of vinyl glue without worrying about the effect because, when it dries, it will become transparent. As for the shapes, you can help them to adhere to the curved surfaces by making a lot of tiny cuts around the edges and then flattening the shapes well with the paintbrush.

NOTES ON WHAT YOU NEED: Rubber boots for children or fun-loving adults. The cuttings come from a sheet of matt-finished wrapping paper.

What you need:
- pair of rubber
  boots
- wrapping paper
  with pictures
  of dogs
- small and medium-
  blade scissors
- vinyl glue
- small flat
  paintbrush
  for the glue
- aluminium
  container
  for the glue
- gloss boat varnish
- flat paintbrush
  for the varnish
- turpentine

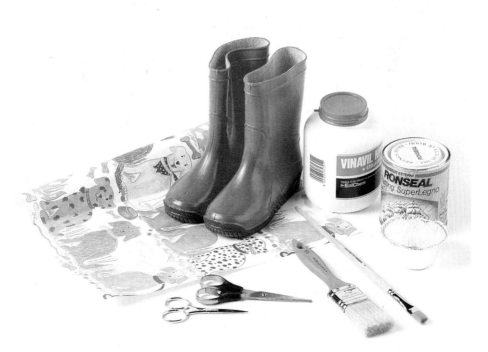

Cut out the pictures
of dogs and the
other designs
on the wrapping
paper.

Glue the backs
of your cuttings
and start to position
them on the boots,
also putting a thick
layer of glue on top
of the pictures.

So that the pictures can follow the curves of the boots, make a lot of tiny cuts around the edges of the paper and smooth them down with the brush.

When the glue is completely dry (this will take several hours since the layer of glue is very thick), apply the first coat of varnish. After 5 or 6 hours you can apply a second coat and you could add a third coat later if necessary. It is a good idea to protect the boots as much as possible since they must be waterproof.

LAMPSHADE

METHOD: Second mixed
method
OBJECT: Lampshade
MATERIAL: Stiff cotton material

CHARACTERISTICS OF THE MATERIAL: Cotton is another unlikely material
for decoupage, but the magic of vinyl glue allows even this type of surface
to be covered.
Of course, the material must be fully stretched.
Cutting out the Victorian silhouettes may be rather difficult but the final
effect is worth all the trouble. This English style of decoupage was very
popular at the beginning of this century.

NOTES ON WHAT YOU NEED: An old cotton lampshade. The Victorian
silhouettes were photocopied
from a book.

What you need:
- cotton lampshade
- photocopies
  of Victorian
  silhouettes
- small scissors
- cutter
- vinyl glue
- small flat
  paintbrush
  for the glue
- aluminium
  container
  for the glue
- satin-finish spray
  varnish

Cut out the Victorian silhouettes with great care, using both a cutter and small scissors.

Spread the glue on the back of the figures and attach them to the lampshade.

*Spread the glue over
the design and over
the whole surface
of the lampshade.*

*When the material is
completely dry, spray
with transparent
varnish. After half
an hour you can
spray with a second
coat of varnish.*

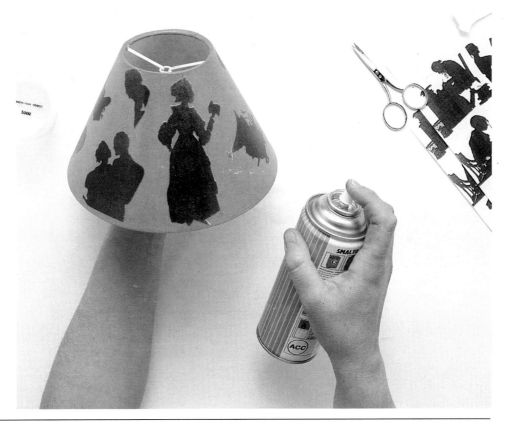

GLASS DISH

METHOD: Second mixed method
OBJECT: Dish
MATERIAL: Clear glass

CHARACTERISTICS OF THE MATERIAL: Decoupage under glass is a variation of the techniques that we have already seen. In fact, the photographs are stuck to the underside of the glass and are visible through the clear glass surface. It is a good idea to use photocopies or paper which is not printed on the back for the pictures.

NOTES ON WHAT YOU NEED: A glass dish or tray. The pictures are colour photocopies of old family photographs. They were made in colour to reproduce the typical effect of photographs considerably yellowed with age.

What you need:
- clear glass dish
- colour or black-and-white photocopies of old family photographs
- small scissors
- cutter
- vinyl glue
- small flat paintbrush for the glue
- aluminium container for the glue
- black gloss spray varnish

When you have cut out the photocopies, spread the glue on the front of the pictures.

Attach them to the bottom of the plate and make small cuts around the edges of the photographs to help them adhere to the curved surface of the plate.

With the brush
and glue, flatten
the paper so that
it adheres perfectly
to the glass. Make
sure that there are
no air bubbles.

When the glue is
completely dry, spray
(after protecting
your work surface
and in a well-aired
environment)
with black gloss
varnish to protect
and finish
the underside
of the plate.

IDEAS

A small round table covered with cuttings of enlarged photocopies of optical designs. The cuttings have been randomly placed and overlapped. The protective varnish is satin-finished because a very shiny surface would not be suitable for this subject.
Method: Second mixed method.

An octagonal card table covered with cuttings of reproductions with tartan motifs taken from a book on the subject. Applied at random, these cuttings form geometrical designs on the table, making a kind of kaleidoscope of Scottish-style designs.
Method: Paintbrush.

This beige ceramic dish has similar decorations to those used for the box on the next page.
The light colouring of the base of the dish is ideal, since the yellowing of the varnish, which often occurs with ageing, will not be noticeable.
Method: Paintbrush.

An oval box in rough cardboard. The decoupage has been made with wrapping paper cuttings showing architectural subjects and with photocopies of baroque decorations. Rough cardboard, like untreated wood, is one of the most suitable surfaces for the blending of decoupage motifs. Warning: Spread a large amount of glue all over the surface, otherwise the varnish may come into contact with the rough cardboard and damage it permanently with grease marks. Method: Paintbrush.

A writing desk set covered with wrapping paper printed with writing motifs and photographs of pens and nibs cut out from magazines. This object derives its main interest from the photographs; otherwise, it would be nothing more than a writing desk set covered in wrapping paper. Pens are often publicised in magazines, like perfume and clocks, and are therefore easy to obtain in large quantities. Method: Paintbrush.

The paperknife, which was part of an ordinary office set, is decorated with decoupage and the edges are finished with black gloss paint.

The writing folder has been covered with a patchwork of overlapping letters and envelopes. In order to prevent creasing and to help the cuttings to lie flat, a large pile of heavy books was placed on top of writing folder for one night.

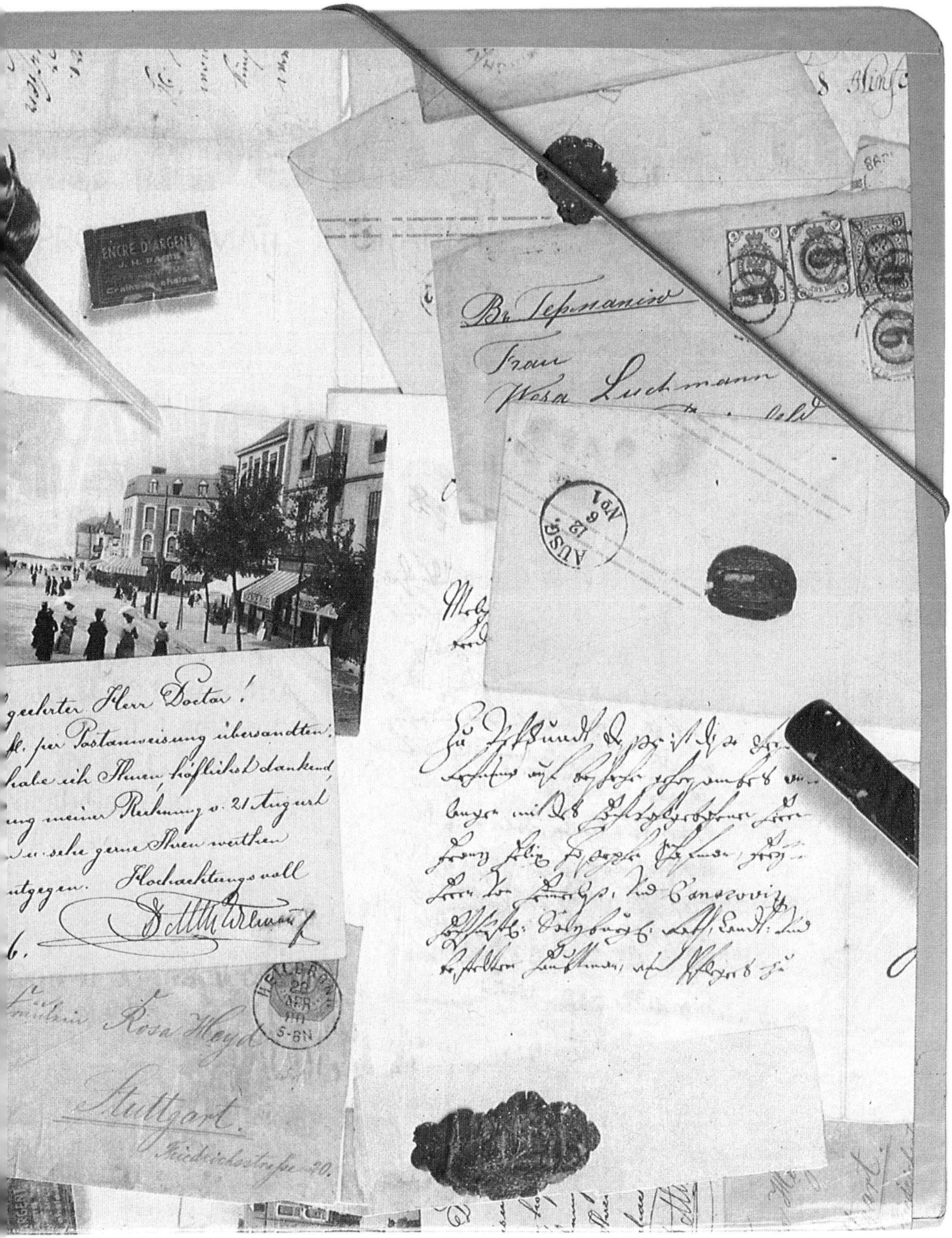
ENCRE D'ARGENT
Frau
Stuttgart

The wooden pencil box was bought at a flea market. After covering and finishing it with black gloss, an old fountain pen, also decorated with decoupage, was attached to the lid as a kind of handle.

The magnifying glass has also been covered with tiny pieces of paper and finished with gloss paint.

This file has been given a new lease of life with decoupage. The design plays on the overlapping of old letters and envelopes and cuttings of photographs of pens and biros.

Can you see what the pen holder originally contained? It was a tea canister. One of the magical properties of decoupage is to transform everyday objects. This pen holder has also been finished with black gloss paint, applied with a fine round-tipped brush.

A pair of white oval
porcelain trays with
a design of cuttings
of photographs
of cutlery taken
from newspapers
and magazines.
This is a highly
original way
of decorating trays

*to use when serving
or simply as wall
decoration.
Obviously, hot
dishes cannot be
placed on the trays
because they would
alter the varnished
surface.
Method: Paintbrush.*

A pair of white porcelain dishes decorated with marine motifs of fishes and shells photocopied onto white and yellow paper. Here one can appreciate the strategy of photocopies on

*coloured paper
to give a highly
original effect.
For the finishing,
a few drops
of liquid gold
paint have been
added to the varnish
to give it a shiny
but veiled effect.
Method: Paintbrush.*

A late nineteenth century wooden table finished with shellac. Floral decoration has been added using cuttings from newspapers, wrapping paper and postcards. This is an excellent solution for attractive old furniture which is not important enough to merit money spent on restoration. In this way glass marks, cracks in the wood and any other defects can be covered and the characteristics of the object can be emphasized.
Method: The pictures have been applied using the paintbrush method, but walnut-coloured wood polish (2 or 3 coats), applied with a cloth, has been used instead of varnish.

Beautiful Christmas baubles decorated with Victorian designs and finished with gilded spray paint. This typical Christmas design needs a lot of patience, but the result is very effective. Cuttings of lighter paper can also be used. In fact, these Victorian designs are rather thick and a little difficult to fold.
Method: Second mixed method.

Two decorative eggs covered in gold leaf and decorated with photocopies of baroque decorations and Victorian figures. The eggs are wooden and can be found in sewing shops. They are old-fashioned mending eggs which have been transformed into richly decorated objects to treasure. Method: Paintbrush.

Coloured candles decorated with colour photocopies of flowers and ribbons. This is perhaps one of the most original uses for decoupage. It is not particularly difficult and allows you to decorate candles for a dinner, perhaps following the theme of the evening or of the menu. An excellent idea for Christmas presents. Method: Second mixed method.

A small tray in white porcelain, decorated with colour photocopies of Victorian figures and flowers.
The photocopies come from a beautiful book on Italian fashion-plates and advertisements from the beginning of this century. Obviously, not being able to use the pages of the book itself, the best solution is to use colour photocopies. Method: Paintbrush.

A milk jug in white porcelain, decorated with flowers taken from magazines. Combined with the tray the effect is very attractive and delicate. The collage of flowers on the smooth curved surface of the porcelain needs a little care. Method: Paintbrush.

A water sprinkler for plants in stiff plastic decorated with wrapping paper cuttings in a leaf design. This is another application of decoupage on an original type of surface. An ordinary water sprinkler, kept in the living room to water indoor plants, is very useful but rather unsightly. This could be a solution. Method: Paintbrush with satin-finish varnish.

This small chocolate tray in white porcelain decorated with cuttings of flowers from magazines makes a lovely companion to the jug. Gardening magazines are a very useful source of floral pictures, generally very well photographed. For this type of decoupage care in choosing the proportions in the composition of the decoration is essential. Method: Paintbrush.

This box (originally containing detergent) is transformed into a container for shoe-brushes and polish. It is decorated with photographs of shoes from fashion magazines.

Another everyday object transformed into a container that can be put on display. The base has been sprayed with silver paint. Method: Second mixed method.

shoe cream
Crème pour chaussures

Crème pour chaussures – shoecreme – schutzcreme
per calzature – crema para el calzado – skocreme
Made in Britain. Fabriqué en Grande Bretagne.
Reckitt Shoecare Products, Hull.
Export Distributors
Reckitt & Colman (Overseas) Ltd.
Meltonian is a Trademark.

A terracotta plate for perfumes. Made with photographs of advertisements for perfume cut out from magazines. For this object the most amusing idea is to find photographs of the same perfumes that will be placed on the dish to create trompe-l'oeil decoupage. Method: Paintbrush.

A wooden 1950s chair covered with photocopies of musical scores, aged with gilded spray paint.
The difficulty lies in covering the legs and the horizontal bars, which are small and round.

Warning: Cut the paper into lots of strips to be applied askew. Use a lot of glue, which you need to strengthen the structure of the chair, if it is very old and a little unstable.
Method: Paintbrush.

An oval box in rough cardboard with a mock leather finish. It was painted with a base of acrylic dark Bordeaux red paint and then little angels and borders photocopied from a book on beige paper were added. The mock leather is a refined finishing technique. It is not difficult to produce. It is important to find the right shade of paint. Several coats of bees-wax will then automatically create the effect. Method: Paint glue and white wax finishing to substitute the varnish.

A small wooden casket covered with gold leaf and decorated with photocopied baroque medallions and scrolls. The gilding technique, now made much easier by new products on the market which are quicker to use, is ideal for adding elegance to even the most ordinary box. This was a rough wooden box originally designed to contain free samples.
Method: Paintbrush.

A round balsawood box with a delightful fruit design made from wrapping paper. The paper is particularly suitable since it is rough (uncoated) and has a design of separate branches so that the composition can be made by overlapping the pictures. Method: Paintbrush.

A round balsawood box decorated with wrapping paper cuttings of printed angels. A teaspoon of gold powder paint, which can be found in any paint shop, has been added to the varnish. You can also mix liquid metallic paints with the varnish or one or two drops of coloured paint to produce a veiled effect. Be careful to check the compatibility of the paints, which must always be synthetic or oil-based. *Method: Paintbrush.*

ENGLISH STYLE

The most traditional and refined decoupage decorations are certainly produced in what is known as the English style. This is created on furniture and objects, generally hand-painted through the application of paper decorations showing scrolls, bows, elaborate picture frames and copies of nineteenth-century ink drawings. The cuttings are stuck but the surface is not protected with fixatives or glue. Many coats of shellac are applied as a finish, which penetrates the paper, giving it an aged effect. In England sheets of Baroque decorations are sold specifically for decoupage designs. An excellent alternative are photocopies from books (specialist publishers can also easily be found). This particular type of print can be found in many types of books since the fashion for this kind of decoration goes back to the second half of the eighteenth century. English aristocrats, returning from their travels abroad, mostly in France and Italy, loved to decorate the antechamber of their libraries with prints reproducing the places and monuments that they had visited to create print rooms. The prints were attached directly to the walls, without frames or glass, but framed on the borders with paper decorated with scrolls and acanthus leaves. The objects in this part of the book are made in this style, which is very elegant, but not difficult to produce.

A wooden tray with scalloped edges painted using a marbling technique. An oval paper decoupage with a mythological subject has been added in the centre and the whole thing is finished in shellac. Refined cuttings and prints suit objects decorated using refined or skilled techniques for the background. The mock stone effect (marbling) is one of these. There is a special technique for producing this effect but, for those who wish to try, it is mainly based on long and careful observation of real marble, followed by a lot of practice with a paintbrush and colours.

A pair of frames in shaped wood sponged with acrylic colours and decorated with cuttings on baroque and neo-classical themes. The frames are made in fairly thick multi-layered plywood and shaped with an electric saw. Decorated wooden buttons have been applied in the four corners and gilded using the gold leaf technique.

This is an alternative frame. The same shape and thickness have been used, but with finer paper decorations. Cutting out these paper shapes requires real skill.

A coat hanger in wood painted with acrylic paints decorated with paper decoupage of festoons and acanthus leaves. Display coat hangers are an excellent idea for small entrances with no wardrobe. This one is particularly refined. Bases applied with opaque acrylic paint are always in pale colours, or shades dirtied with umber or ivory.

A knitting needle box or tie box. Painted with acrylic colours and decorated with water-coloured paper cuttings. In this case, as in other similar cases, the paper has simply been stuck on, without then protection of a glue covering. This allows you to appreciate the water-colouring of the prints much more, even though it makes the object a little more delicate.

A pair of wooden chairs in white and green gloss paint. The backs are decorated with borders and scrolls, unprotected by varnishing.

The decoupage decoration, entirely carried out on the chair backs, has a characteristic double chain of pearls, which follows the contours of the wooden scroll.

A decorative ball with decoupage appliqués of scrolls and acanthus leaves and finished with shellac.
This is a beautiful object for a bookshelf or a desk. Originally these balls were only made of precious marble, crystal or hard stone. This decoupage idea is even more refined. The paper scrolls help the paper to adhere to the curved surface without having to perform small cuts usually needed to make the paper fit difficult surfaces.

Bellows in shaped
wood painted
in tempera
and decorated
with paper friezes.
This is a small
masterpiece
of composition
and decoupage.
All the friezes are
carefully balanced
to suit the shape
and basic colouring
of the bellows.

A pair of wooden boxes painted in acrylic colours and given paper decorations with pictures of butterflies and cherubs. They have both been finished with shellac. The main difficulty of the English style lies in the composition of the themes,

which works if the proportions of the figures are well-balanced, especially since in this type of decoration there is no over-lapping. The butterfly theme is very common in English decoupage. These have been aged with many layers of liquid shellac.

A wooden box covered in gold leaf. The paper decorations have a baroque theme. The gold background is one of the most suitable for this style of decoupage.

This was once a costly and time-consuming technique, kept secret by goldsmiths. Now there are rapid glues and metal sheeting, substituting the gold nugget.

A shaped wooden mantelpiece clock, painted in acrylic colours, decorated with cuttings and baroque pictures and finished with shellac. A classic for the walls of a study or library. The base, already painted, can be aged further with cotton wool lightly dipped in a liquid bituminous ageing solution.

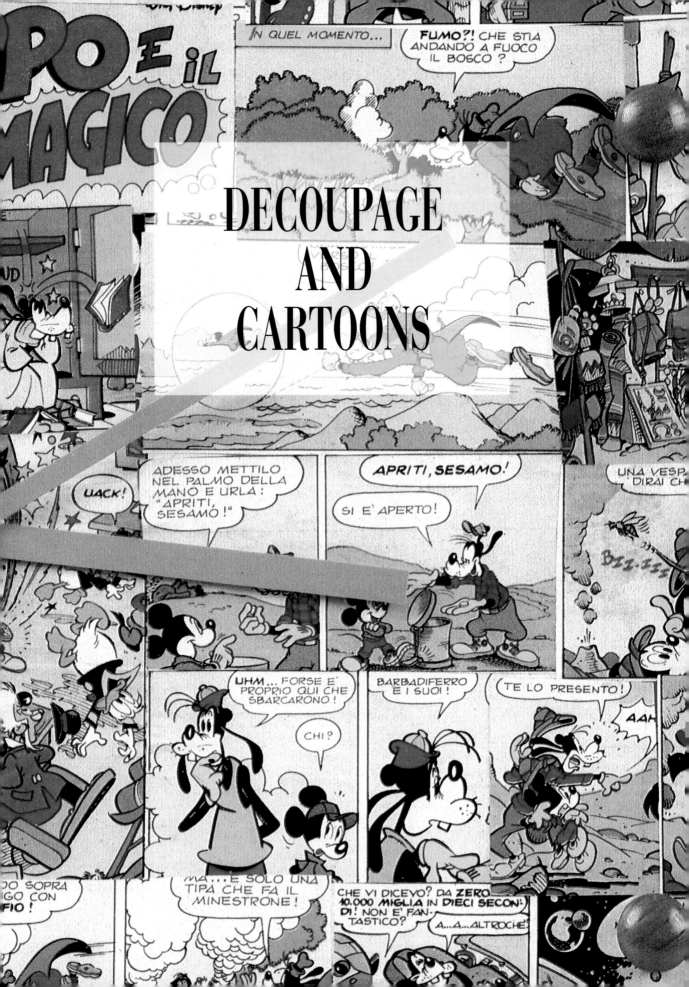

DECOUPAGE
AND
CARTOONS

Using cartoons is a very attractive way of producing decoupage. You do not need to be an expert in cutting or applying, because the pages can be used whole. The objects in these photographs have been made with a variation of the paintbrush method, using wallpaper glue instead of vinyl glue and fixative instead of varnish. This system is recommended for those who do not wish to waste time on the composition of the cuttings. The cartoon pages can be cut out and overlapped without taking particular care, a little like the pages of musical scores. Moreover, large surfaces can be covered, such as furniture, doors or walls. Imagine a metre-long strip around the walls of a child's bedroom.

This large wall clock is covered with bright and cheerful cartoon pictures. Coloured wooden semicircles have been attached to show the numbers of the hours, which can be found in haberdashery shops. Even the quartz movements for the clocks can be easily and cheaply obtained.

A folding garden chair in wood completely covered in pages from the Italian version of the Donald Duck cartoons.
This is an example of how any type of surface can be covered. Making the cuttings fit the chair legs perfectly needs a lot of patience, but the result is exceedingly attractive. The real challenge would be to make a dozen of these chairs, to use for summer evening meals on the terrace or in the garden.

A table or wall picture frame for photographs, covered with pages from the Italian version of the Donald Duck cartoons.
In contrast with what was said about decorating with cartoons, the composition of the decoupage design on the frame has been very carefully planned. Objects can be designed and read in this way when they are as small as this one.

AMERICAN STYLE

The American taste for juxtaposing and combining highly-coloured pictures, already in vogue in the 1950s, is very well-known. The photographed objects on these pages were made in New Mexico, in the south of the United States. The method is similar to the paintbrush method. Vinyl glue is spread under and over the pictures and then many coats of transparent varnish are applied, perhaps as many as 10 or 12 coats. The pictures used to decorate these objects are highly characteristic. Some have even been made with labels from tomato or onion soup cans clearly mixed with advertisements of Florida and Arizona. Generally, the objects used for this style of decoration are not precious. In fact, rough wood is used for the appliqués, varnished only after the collage has been completed.

A rectangular
wooden picture
frame.
A large frame
produced by paying
great attention
to the composition
of the cuttings,
balancing the
colours as well as
the dimensions.
This would also be
ideal for a mirror
frame.

A low bench in rough wood. The same decorations and finish have been used here as for the clothes hanger. This seems to be the poor cousin of the refined sitting room foot-rests that have recently come back into fashion. This example, however, has the advantage of being original and covered with a high-quality decoupage.

A wall clothes hanger in rough wood with flower and fruit decorations. Finished with jute cord. The finishing is in keeping with the country style of the object. Even the cord has been painted and fixed with transparent varnish.

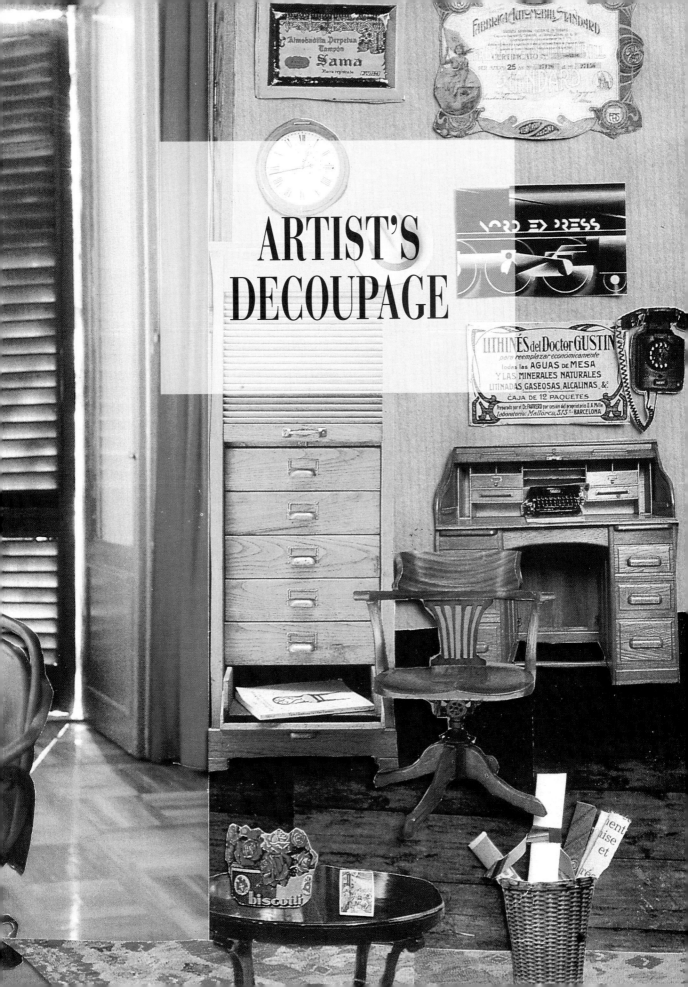

ARTIST'S DECOUPAGE

The whole of this book has been based on objects of everyday or decorative use, but which are still recognizable objects. Decoupage is, however, also exploited as an artistic technique. Artists are, in fact, always in search of original modes of expression. Collage forms part of this technique as much as oil painting and water-colours.

I have chosen to finish with some works by an extremely gifted artist who, using only the modern magazines found in any newsagent's, manages to create truly magical environments and atmospheres. Always playing on the factors of the proportions of the pictures, she manages to create perspective, a sense of depth and three-dimensional space.

She also has an eye for detail: objects and the smallest hidden things, only noticeable when one enters these works with imaginative eyes. It almost looks like an experiment, in decoupage, of virtual reality. Some pieces are real paper miniatures that the artist composes with great taste and elegance. This is yet another example of how many infinite creative possibilities can be inspired by the simple, but fascinating technique of decoupage.

Liliana Castellaneta, 1993, Doll's House, 80 x 40 cm.

Liliana Castellaneta,
1994, Spring Hours,
27 x 27 cm.

Liliana Castellaneta,
*1994, Small Pink
Theatre, 33 x 27 cm.*

Liliana Castellaneta,
*1993, The Publicity
Studio, 40 x 30 cm.*

Liliana Castellaneta,
*1994, The Milliner's
Studio, 40 x 30 cm.*

DECORATIONS
FOR
DECOUPAGE

LAIRD'S
BLOOM OF YOUTH
AND WHITE LILAC SOAP

Beautify your Complexion

To my Darling

JULY

S M T W T F S

Charming Cloe.

The Words by Mr Jersey.

Set by Mr Gladwin.

When charming Cloe gently walks, Or sweetly Smiles, or gayly talks,

No Goddess can with her compare, So Sweet her Look, so soft her Air.

Bickham Sculp

ACKNOWLEDGEMENTS

To all those who have helped me, who have lent objects given to them and who have contributed to the success of this book.

To my sister Mariaserena. To my friend Gianna. To my friend Manola. To my friend Marco Magheri (Poggio a Caiano) for all the objects he produced in wood. To my student and contributor Deborah Aguiari, who produced many of the objects photographed in the Ideas chapter. To Mary Bellentani, who produces the English style decoupage for her decorative shop Quadrature in Milan. She has created all the objects photographed in this chapter. To the Milanese artist Liliana Castellaneta, who has kindly lent examples of her work. To Ornella at the Studio Karibu for the objects decorated with decoupage from Mickey Mouse and Donald Duck. To the Fiorucci shop in Milan for the objects in the chapter on American style decoupage.

To the companies that have kindly lent me the material that I chose to use for the production of my objects: VISUAL BOOKS (for the Dover books), Milan; IMBALLAGGI GIPPONI (for wrapping paper), Milan; MARK SERVICE (for Ronseal varnish), Milan; GIUSEPPE CAMBIAGHI S.p.A. (for thinners and turpentine), Milan; TALKEN COLOR (for spray paints and varnishes), Legnano (Milan); 3M ITALIA S.p.A. (for spray glue), Segrate (Milan); F.LLI MAIMERI (for acrylic paints and varnishes), Bettolino di Mediglia (Milan); ADIT TALENS (for acrylic paints and varnishes), Sesto Ulteriano (Milan).

I particularly wish to thank Piero Baguzzi and all the other people at the photographic studios who have patiently had to suffer my work in progress, that is, my live work with glue, paints and spray.

Photos: Piero Baguzzi

Graphics and paging: Paola Masera and Amelia Verga